"Finally a children's book that takes a gentle and thoughtful exploration into blended families. A great book for teachers and counselors to use with children."
    —Susan M. Kuczura, Psy.D.
      Licensed Psychologist

"Ellis-Berg explores the complex emotions of the blended family in a thought provoking way. Counselors, teachers, and parents will find the conversation starters they need to facilitate healthy conversations to help children talk about and come to understand their new family."
    —Dr. Mark Loiterman, M.Ed., Ph.D.

BELL Meets the B.EL.L. Pack!

BELL
Meets the B.EL.L. Pack!

Written by Carrie Ellis-Berg

Illustrated by Corry Damey

BELL PACK LLC
Chesapeake, Virginia

Copyright © 2016 by Bell Pack LLC

All rights reserved No part of this book may be reproduced in any form or by any electronic or mechanical means, including information storage and retrieval systems, without permission in writing from the copyright owner, except by a reviewer, who may quote brief passages in a review. Scanning, uploading and electronic distribution of this book or the facilitation of such without permission of the copyright owner is prohibited. Please purchase only authorized electronic editions, and do not participate in or encourage electronic piracy of copyrighted materials. Your support of the rights of the author, and other creative artists, is appreciated. Any member of educational institutions wishing to photocopy part of this work for classroom use, or anthology, should send inquiries to the publisher at the address set forth below.

ISBN: 9780997379600

Library of Congress Control Number: 2016903672

Published by Bell Pack LLC. Contact via Bellpackllc@gmail.com

Cover and interior text design and layout by Stephen Tiano, Book Designer

*To my crazy B.EL.L Pack—An endless source of inspiration and happiness
I love you all!*

On a warm, sunny, summer day, I ran all around the farm searching for my favorite bone.

I sniffed and ran, and I ran and sniffed.

It has to be here somewhere!

I closed my eyes and followed my nose until my nose ran right into a big, smelly pair of boots. *Ooops! Those are Master's feet!* I looked up with my cutest, sorriest face. He was not alone!

> Activity:
> See if you and your child can find the bell hidden in each picture ... there's one in every scene, but it might be tough to spot!

"These are your new owners," he said. I could see a very excited looking couple. *You'd think they've never been to a farm before, or maybe they've just never seen a puppy as beautiful as I am.*

But new owners?! I didn't ask for new owners! And that one—that one is freakishly tall!

"Hello puppy!" the woman squealed. She had a very squeaky voice. She knelt down and gently smoothed back my ears, and it felt good.

Hmmm. They seem pretty nice, and she does pet me just the way I like. They can't be too bad, I guess. I'll go check it out. It's not like I'm ever going to find my bone here anyway.

Before I knew what was happening, I was in the back of their car, and we were on our way.

I wonder what my new farm will be like. I wonder if they have kids and if they'll like me. All of this thinking is making me sleepy.

With that I closed my eyes and drifted off to sleep.

I woke up when the car turned down a bumpy gravel driveway. I rubbed my eyes and sat up to look out of the window. We had pulled into a silly looking place, way too small to be a proper farm.

"Here's your new home, Pup," Tall Man said.

Huh? This is not a farm. This is just a house. I need room, people! Have you seen my size lately? I don't want to be here! I need space—room to move!

"Wait 'til you meet Buster!" squealed the lady with a squeaky voice.

And just as I spun around to jump back into the car, up came a little Terrier, yapping and snapping at me!

Oh great! This silly little rat must be Buster.

"Hi! I'm Buster!" he exclaimed. "I'm a dog—just like you."

"You can't be a dog!" I argued. "You're *waaaay* too small!"

Buster laughed and said, "I promise I'm a dog. So are you. You just happen to be the size of a horse! What's your name?"

"I'm Puppy," I said proudly, puffing out my chest.

"Yeah, I know, I know. But what's your name?" Buster asked again.

"I just told you!" I said firmly. "I'm *Puppy*!"

"Oh, c'mon, you have to have a real name," stated Buster. "If not, you're about to get one!"

I don't want a new silly name! Who does this rat think he is?

"Where am I, anyway?" I asked, trying to change the subject.

"You are at the Brooks-Ellison-Littleton's House!" explained Buster with excitement. His tail wagged even faster.

"What's the Brooks-Ellison-Littleton's House?"

"They are my family, and I am guessing they're yours now, too. They are super nice and super fun. But the most special thing about them is that they are a *blended* family," he replied.

I asked, "What's a *blended* family?"

> *Discussion:*
> Before reading on, ask your child what they think a "blended family" is. What might be good about being part of a blended family? What might be hard?

Buster, with a serious look on his face, said quietly, "It's when there are two families with two sets of parents who can't live together anymore, and they get a divorce. Then one of the mommies marries the other daddy, and they live together with the kids."

"I'm confused," I said. My head hurt thinking about all these people in such a small space.

"It can be really confusing," he continued. "There are four kids, so there is a lot of noise and a lot of fun. Mom has two kids from her first marriage, and their names are Ashton and Matthew. Dad has two kids, too, and their names are Daniel and Georgia. They are each very special in their own way."

Right then the front door flew open, and four crazy, squealing kids came running in. I closed my eyes and braced myself for the impact.

"A new dog!" shouted Daniel.

"Wow!" exclaimed Matthew.

"I love her!" squealed Georgia.

Ashton shouted, "A new best friend for Buster!"

> *Discussion:*
> How do you think Puppy might be feeling right now? Talk to your child about how they felt meeting their new family for the first time.

Daniel was the first to ask, "What's her name?"

"We were waiting for you guys to help name her," said Squeaky Lady.

"How about Rex?" asked Matthew.

"Or Lexi!" yelled Georgia.

"I like Layla!" shouted Ashton.

> *Discussion:*
> Sometimes children—and parents too—in blended families have several different nicknames. Talk to your child about this—some children love it; others can find it confusing!

"I have an idea," Tall Man said. "Why don't we take the first letter of each of all of our last names and turn it into a name?"

"B for Brooks!" said Daniel.

"L for Littleton," shouted Matthew.

"Don't forget E!" interrupted Mom. "E for Ellison!"

"I got it! B – E – L! Bell! How about Bell?!" Tall Man asked everyone.

"That's awesome!" everyone yelled with excitement.

Daniel asked me, "What do you think, *Bell*?"

"Woof!" I said. "Woof!!!" *I really did think this was a great name and so much better than Puppy.*

And suddenly I heard the words that changed this family's name forever. "Our family can be called the B.EL.L. Pack!" shouted Ashton. "If you take everyone's last name blended together like we did to make up Bell's name, it's just like us! We're a blended family."

Everyone loved the idea, and so did I.

> *Activity:*
> Take some of the letters from your families' names and see what words you and your child can make. Can you come up with a fun nickname for your "pack"?

After a few days of fun and chaos, I took some time to reflect on my time here with the B.EL.L Pack.

I am soooo lucky to be a part of this blended family. I wonder what I can do to show them how much I love them?

I know! Each night Squeaky Lady and Tall Man go in and tuck each kid in at night. Maybe I should start doing that, too. The children seem to really like my kisses!

That night, I went in to see the oldest, Ashton. He was in bed snuggling up with Buster. I took a big running jump, leapt into the air and WHUMP! I landed right on top of them!

"Bell!" Ashton cried, "You're way too big to be on the bed!" Buster rolled his eyes and buried his head under his paws. *He really doesn't know how to have fun!*

Who should I visit next? I wondered as I stood in the hallway, looking at all the doors. I know. I'll go visit cute, little Georgia. She has some very cuddly stuffed animals, and maybe she will let me use one for my sleepy time.

I took another big running jump and WHUMP! I landed right on top of her.

"Bell!" she shouted. "You're way too big to be on the bed!"

Next I'll go visit Daniel. He always sneaks treats upstairs.

I took another big running jump and WHUMP! I landed right on top of him.

"Bell!" he shouted. "You're way too big to be on the bed!"

I snatched a cookie and ran out the door.

All of a sudden I heard a crying sound coming from Matthew's room.

Why is he so sad?

I walked slowly into his room and gently climbed into his bed. I licked, and licked, and licked, covering Matthew with slobbery kisses. That *had* to cheer him up. This time I decided not to run out the door. Instead I lay down and snuggled up close to him, thinking he could really use a friend.

Discussion:
Often bedtime can be a difficult time for children in blended families. For many children, it can feel like they are always sleeping in a strange place. What can you and your child do to make sleeping in different homes easier?

And just like that, he began to talk. "Bell, I am so sad. *I used to be the baby, but I'm not the baby anymore. Georgia gets so much more attention than I do!*"

I am so sad for him. Blended families don't seem like fun at all. I know, I'll go get Buster. He'll know what to do.

I crept down the hall and went into Ashton's room.

"Buster!" I whispered. "Buster!" I said a little louder. "Buster!" I bellowed.

"Horse, can't you see I'm sleeping? Sheesh! What's your problem?!" he snapped.

"Come here!" I said. "I need to talk to you."

"So what's the trouble?"

"Well, I decided I was going to show everyone the love that they have shown for me, so I went room to room and loved them up. Then I heard crying coming from Matthew's room, and I climbed in his bed to snuggle. He started telling me about how he doesn't get attention like he used to and how Georgia really is the littlest now. It made me feel really sad for him, and it made me wonder if this whole blending thing was a good idea."

Buster looked up at me and started to explain. "I remember when Ashton and Matthew's parents were together. It was hard, and sometimes the kids felt it. Now that Dad and Mom are married they are much happier, and so are the kids. The kids even tell me of all the fun they have at the other houses. And how can I forget—they get more birthday and Christmas gifts!"

"Sure that sounds fine and all, but I am really worried about Matthew," I started to say, but Buster interrupted me. "Siblings will fight. Think about when you were at the farm. Didn't you fight with your brothers and sisters?" asked Buster.

"Of course," I said. "I definitely had some fights, especially with Bob. He smacked me and yelled at me every day," I stated very emphatically. I could relate to Matthew now.

"See?" Buster said, "Blended families are just like regular families. Just a lot more love to give. It's like double the love. The parents have the hardest job though. They have to try really hard not to play favorites and not show more love to one child than the other. Thankfully, Mom and Dad are really good at making each child feel special. They love each one—including their stepchildren—just like they are their own. They know that's the most important part of being in a blended family."

"I believe it," I said.

Suddenly we heard footsteps upstairs. We both ran to the stairs and saw Tall Man and Squeaky Lady together tucking each kid in bed and telling them they love them. We watched as they came into Matthew's room and asked what was wrong. I heard Matthew say the same words that he had said to me. I watched as they held him tightly and whispered the words, "We love you, and no matter what, you can always count on us to listen and help."

Matthew seemed to love having his mom and his stepdad whisper those words, and with that Buster said, "This is why these parents are so special. They love *all* of these children all the way to the moon and back a billion times, and then a few times more."

> *Activity:*
> Help your children to recognize fairness and equality. Take the time to sit down as a family and ask each child to write down the times they felt special. For example, it might be an activity they got to do, something you or a sibling said to them, or something they were helped with.

We went back downstairs to find a snack, and I thought about today and the time that I had with the B.EL.L. Pack.

Then I remembered that the kids have other parents.

"When do the kids go to their other parents' houses?" I asked.

"Tomorrow," Buster said. "They leave every other weekend."

"Oh no!" I cried. "That's terrible!"

No silly! It's not terrible!" he said. "They love going to the other parents' houses. They would be so sad if they didn't." "Yeah, I guess you are right," I said. "If they have this much love at the other house, too, I can see why they'd want to go."

"Cheer up, Bell!" Buster exclaimed, giving me a little shove. I looked down at him—maybe he wasn't so bad after all.

Buster wagged his tail, and his eyes started to light up. "Now that we have each other, we can have some crazy adventures! There have been some things I've wanted to do around here for a while. Now that I have you and your mighty size, we can do some really BIG things!"

I smiled to myself, put my head down, closed my eyes, and went to sleep. All I could hear was Buster starting to snore. This just might not be too bad after all ...

About the Author

Carrie Ellis-Berg has been an elementary teacher for ten years. Together as a blended family, she and her husband have four children. They live in Virginia with their two dogs and a snake.

Watch for the continuing adventures
of The B.EL.L. Pack
in *Bell and the Great, Big Mess*

www.ingramcontent.com/pod-product-compliance
Lightning Source LLC
LaVergne TN
LVHW071025070426
835507LV00002B/34